Teach Kids How to Think

7 Secrets for Raising Intelligent Children With a Strong Mentality and Positive Mindset

Frank Dixon

Before we begin, I have something special waiting for you. An action-packed 1 page printout with a few quick & easy tips taken from this book that you can start using today to become a better parent right now!

It's my gift to you, free of cost. Think of it as my way of saying thank you to you for purchasing this book.

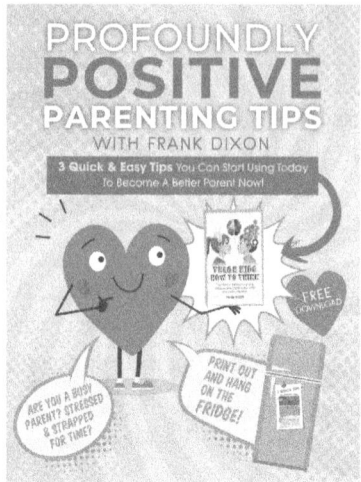

Claim your download of Profoundly Positive Parenting with Frank Dixon by scanning the QR code below and join my mailing list.

Sign up below to grab your free copy, print it out and hang it on the fridge!

Sign Up By Scanning The QR Code With Your Phone's Camera To Be Redirected To A Page To Enter Your Email And Receive INSTANT Access To Your Download

Before we jump in, I'd like to express my gratitude. I know this mustn't be the first book you came across and yet you still decided to give it a read. There are numerous courses and guides you could have picked instead that promise to make you an ideal and well-rounded parent while raising your children to be the best they can be.

But for some reason, mine stood out from the rest and this makes me the happiest person on the planet right now. If you stick with it, I promise this will be a worthwhile read.

In the pages that follow, you're going to learn the best parenting skills so that your child can grow to become the best version of themselves and in doing so experience a meaningful understanding of what it means to be an effective parent.

Notable Quotes About Parenting

"Children Must Be Taught How To Think, Not What To Think."

— Margaret Mead

"It's easier to build strong children than to fix broken men [or women]."

- Frederick Douglass

"Truly great friends are hard to find, difficult to leave, and impossible to forget."

— George Randolf

"Nothing in life is to be feared, it is only to be understood. Now is the time to understand more, so that we may fear less."

— Scientist Marie Curie

Table of Contents

Introduction

A child develops skills the same way a builder builds a house: Its foundation is the most crucial step. Every pillar (value and belief system) has to stand firm. Then come the many rooms and levels that stem from the same pillars. Walls then form rooms (solidification of beliefs through experience and exploration). During its construction, every day is a new sight. Once the foundation has been laid and the pillars are in place, the house seems to come to life in the blink of an eye. All of a sudden, you feel like the house is ready faster than you expected. But then, there are also some days where the view remains the same. Visible or not, be sure that a lot is going on behind the scenes every day.

Children develop skills to critically think and learn in a predictable sequence. It all begins with making up stories by looking at pictures or remembering words and their meanings. But every child can take their own sweet time to develop these skills. These differences are often the result of some inherited tendencies, the amount of exposure and independence they have, or both. Additionally, their environment also stimulates their learning. For example, when they start school, they pick up new things and skills nearly every day.

They learn to converse, make and keep friends, share, and take responsibility.

Parents have a key role to play in nurturing how quickly they pick up great learning and thinking skills. They can help children understand the world around them, encourage exploration, and share their experiences to arouse interest and curiosity to know more.

Many theories are addressing a child's cognitive development, but Jean Piaget's cognitive developmental theory seems to aptly explain how children process thoughts, interact with the world around them, and understand how things work.

Earlier, it was assumed that children thought the same as adults did. Piaget proposed an alternative theory claiming that children think differently than adults. He explained how the development of the mind happens and how thoughts are processed in a child's mind. His cognitive developmental theory divided this development into four steps that happen in a sequential manner stated below (Cherry, 2020):

1. **Sensorimotor Stage:** A period between birth and age two, an infant relies on their sensory perception and motor skills to gain knowledge about the world.

2. **Pre-Operational Stage:** From age two until six, a child explores the world using language. This is when beliefs are formed. At this point, a

child may not fully grasp the logic, manipulate information, or take in the viewpoints of others.

3. **Concrete Operational Stage**: During this period between the ages of seven up to eleven, a child builds command over mental operations and how things work. Children start to think critically and form concrete perceptions about previously abstract concepts.

4. **Formal Operational Stage:** This period from 12 and over is the time when teenagers develop critical thinking skills including deductive reasoning, questioning opinions, and systematic planning. They gain more control over their decisions and learn how manipulation and negotiation improve their odds of getting what they want.

Many parents question the need for raising intelligent children. They believe that all children are gifted uniquely, and only those talents that they are born with should be honed and worked upon. True, we all are beautiful in our ways, and it is our differences that make us stand out, but here's the thing: With the world becoming more and more judgmental, manipulative, and competitive, we need leaders and citizens who question facts that they receive. We need people who would not be fed fake news and lies by politicians and company giants who swear to do good but are also the ones creating boundaries, endorsing hate, and promoting war crimes. We need smart people who will see through the false advertising and be thoughtful. We need adults who will think before making any rash decisions that impact them and the lives of others around them. We need people who won't stand down and will raise their voices for human and women's rights. We need people who will establish healthy boundaries, put an end to the bullying culture in schools and workplaces, and do it confidently. In short, we need to raise men and women who will lead the coming generations toward a happier, greener, and more innovative world.

Learning to think critically and make smart decisions is something that will help young minds throughout their lives. It will help them attain academic success, outshine in their workplaces, and create happy and safe lives for others in their community. When children use analytical thinking skills, they can balance their own needs and the needs of others. They can remain well-formed and not give in to what the media, newspapers, and the internet feed us.

Now is the time to plant the seeds in their mind and expose them to experiences that will help them foster their complex thinking skills.

The goal of this book is to raise a thinker who doesn't only believe in one side of the story but can see through the politicians and media that twist facts to feed their agendas, can hold proper dialogues at dinner tables without becoming offended, question things that they don't think are right, and look after themselves in a better way.

So, let's kick this off and discover the seven secrets to raising a thinker who will change the world!

Chapter 1:

Can We Develop Critical

Thinking Skills?

Some children are subjective thinkers while others are objective. Children with subjective thinking rely on their personal opinions, judgments, interpretations, and emotions. They twist and mold facts to their ease. Subjective thinkers don't care about the importance of theories, facts, scientific data, and objective tools. They make decisions based on their emotional understanding and bias. This is an ill-suited and restrictive approach, as one deliberately avoids seeing things as they are. When emotions get the best of us, our decisions are no longer logic-based and thoughtful ones. They seem right at the moment but cause us to harm in the long run.

Objective thinkers, on the other hand, rely on reasoning, fact-based, observable, and measurable information. Objective thinking is a mental process that takes into account the logical consideration of a topic or situation without any subjective bias. Objective thinkers take informed decisions as they rely on the factual aspect of things. Their decisions are free from any form of prejudice and judgment. Objective thinkers make time for research and only form an opinion or belief about something if they can trace it back to some statistic or fact.

In a world where our children are bombarded with all sorts of negative, biased, and unauthentic messages, it is equally important to raise a child that can see past through all of it and know right from wrong. When young, they may have a hard time evaluating what they see and hear, but as they grow, they develop the skills to form opinions and viewpoints. Being objective and out-of-the-box thinkers, they can excel academically and professionally.

Whatever your child plans to do 10 years from now, critical thinking, problem-solving skills, and objectivity will help them succeed and make the right decisions. Therefore, as a parent, it becomes our duty to encourage children to think for themselves, question everything, and not form solid opinions about anything unless very sure.

You may not realize this now but giving them the right tools that cultivate critical thinking is one of the greatest gifts you can offer. In a rapidly changing world, children need to learn how to take care of themselves without relying on others to dictate to them. They need to be confident enough to choose a lifestyle they find suitable and live up to their values and beliefs. Critical thinking will allow them to make sense of, compare, analyze, contrast, and make inferences about the information they receive from media, newspapers, and editorials.

Science-Backed Benefits of Critical Thinking Skills

Critical and objective thinking skills are a valuable asset for a child, says Dr. Pickerill, a child psychologist. When children are taught to own up to their mistakes, solve complex problems independently, and determine the effect external stimuli have on them, they can deal with the pressures that accompany daily life. From peer pressure to giving in to some information fed to them via a media channel, being themselves and staying true to what they believe in is essential—it builds resilience and sees between the lines. Critical thinkers are better at solving math problems; comparing and contrasting between things; and forming an argument. Critical thinking allows young minds to self-reflect and improves their skill set (Gordon, 2021).

Critical thinking also nurtures creativity, fosters independence, and encourages curiosity. Critical thinkers have tons of questions to ask. They rarely settle for the information they receive. They want to know more about the behind-the-scenes of things and how they work.

Exceptional critical thinking skills also improve the relationship between you and the child. It teaches social skills like how to communicate and state opinions, how to respect boundaries, show empathy, and reduce stress, says Amanda Morin (2019) on the healthcare website, Verywell Mind. She believes that a child who can solve their problems autonomously becomes more confident of their abilities and skills. They become primed to handle whatever life throws their way.

Critical thinking skills also boost creativity, inventiveness, and raise IQ. During an experiment, Richard Herrnstein and his colleagues asked 400 seventh graders to take part in a program. Some students were given explicit instruction in critical thinking via a 45-minute session. The program featured hypothesis testing, evaluation of complex arguments, basic logic, decision making, and inventiveness among other things. After the session, both groups of students were tested on a variety of tasks that included the Raven Progressive Matrices and Otis-Lennon School Ability Test. The results were startling. Compared to the students who didn't receive the session, the students who did showed substantial and statistically significant improvements in inventive thinking, language comprehension, and IQ (Hernstein et al., 1986).

Research also shows that children who lack basic thinking skills tend to have a higher chance of developing behavioral problems as they grow older (Sun & Hui, 2012). This is accurate because children who lack basic critical thinking skills are unable to comprehend things wisely. They believe in what they see and never question things. They stick to what they know and have trouble reshaping their views about anything. Trying to change them makes them angry and frustrated.

When children can think for themselves and form opinions, they can self-reflect on their shortcomings and weaknesses and work on improving them. They can search for ways and strategies to hone their skills and become an expert in them. When speaking with others, they can sense where they are coming from and re-evaluate their arguments to have more informed and fact-based conversations. They can also distinguish between evidence and its interpretation. For example, let's look at the example below and see if you can spot what's wrong with it.

Apple just recently reached two trillion dollars in market capitalization (Bursztynsky, 2020). Despite being one of the biggest companies, it only allows apps that it has approved to be installed on iOS phones. This shows that the company doesn't care about the openness of its platform.

A critical thinker would quickly differentiate between a personal bias and a factual one. The first sentence states the obvious. It can be traced back to authentic sources. The second sentence, however, has a personal opinion attached to it. A common teenager with poor thinking skills may not see it and believe in the opinion of another.

Similarly, in another experimental study, researcher Anat Zohar and his colleague tested the analytical thinking skills of 678 seventh graders. They randomly picked some students to take critical thinking lessons as part of their biology curriculum (Zohar & Tamir, 1993). These students were trained to spot logical fallacies and distinguish between subjective and objective reasoning. Students in the other group learned biology from the same book but without any special training on analytical thinking.

After the program ended, the students were tested again. It was found that the students who took the analytical thinking training showed a significant improvement in their analytical skills and not just biology-related problems. They performed better in the test that involved questions about solving everyday problems (Zohar & Tamir, 1993).

Not having the skills to think and analyze information can lead to it being misconstrued. This can lead to problems at school, in relationships, and at work. Finally, critical thinking promotes open-mindedness and improved observation skills. Children who cultivate these skills within themselves with the help of their teachers and parents can have a deeper understanding of the world and not believe everything that they see.

Chapter 2:

Praise Effort—Not

Intelligence

For centuries, we have been rewarding kids for being the best and brightest as both winners and position holders. We have celebrated their wins with parties and gatherings. We proudly show off their awards and certificates, frame their medals, place their photos on the walls, and remind everyone how great they are. But what about the times when they weren't smart or when they didn't get the grades expected of them? When they lost a match or felt short of finishing up a task? When they received a letter from school for misbehavior? How many of those incidents have we talked about and celebrated?

None.

We haven't done that, and we still don't do it. For us, praising them only matters when they win—not when they perform well. We fail to offer support when despite their best effort, they lose a game, get benched during a match, or make a mistake.

We should, but we don't. This leads to them never understanding the importance of giving it their best shot. The destination isn't always the goal. Sometimes, the journey is more satisfactory. Not encouraging them to give their best and not worry about winning or losing makes them lose their confidence. They start to believe that they will only be valued and loved if they do well. This also prevents them from accepting life's inevitable disappointments and failures. Conversely, praising them for their effort and hard work enhances their confidence in their abilities. They feel more driven and motivated to make progress and ultimately succeed.

In the 1990s, a survey involving parents was conducted. They were asked a series of questions about how they perceive a child's ability and intelligence. As per the results, 85% of parents claimed that praising a child when they do well makes them feel smart. But the findings were different from what the researchers had noticed. They found that praising a child for their intelligence makes them defensive and fragile (Dweck, 2015).

Children who are repeatedly told that they are smart or intelligent are more likely to give up when they don't fare well in a difficult task. They soon give up and become frustrated.

Children who are praised for only their intelligence and not their effort tend to believe that intelligence is a fixed trait (i.e., they either have it or not). Such a belief makes children less willing to accept their mistakes, confront them, and rectify them. This was further experimented in a study published in 1999 comprising 168 freshmen applying to universities in Hong Kong. All the curriculum and coursework were in English. Students who believed that intelligence is an ever-growing trait, despite doing badly in the English test the first time, were more inclined to take a remedial test. On the other hand, students who believed in fixed intelligence and performed poorly the first time were not only unwilling to accept their scores but also less likely to opt for a chance to rectify them (Dweck, 2015).

According to Brian Galvin, chief academic officer and teacher at Varsity Tutors in Seattle, when students receive incentives and rewards on getting good grades and test scores, it doesn't move the needle much. On the other hand, when parents and educators reward enthusiasm, effort, and willingness to attempt new things, students are more likely to keep giving their best and improving.

To help you understand how this can be put to practice, below are some examples —based off a list by Carol Dweck (2015)—that depict how parents can praise effort and hard work:

- "I know we struggled a bit today. Let's talk about it. I'll go first."

- "You did an excellent job painting those faces. They look so real. I am sure you will grow up to become a great artist one day."

- "I am proud of you for giving your best shot. I know how hard you studied for the test, brilliantly outlined the study material, and tested yourself on it several times. It really shows the improvement in your grades."

- "This is awesome that you are trying so many different angles to look at a problem. I am positive you will learn how to solve it."

- "This was one hard application essay, but I am glad that you stuck with it until you were done. That's great dedication."

- "This looks hard but also fun. Let's keep trying until we get it right."

Kicking off conversations in such a manner shows that you are genuinely interested in how they are doing—not just in what they are doing. Praising hard work alongside motivation can boost a child's morale to keep trying. Therefore, make it a habit to encourage action and progress. Never miss a chance to praise them when you catch them trying hard.

Luck Isn't Always on Your Side

The reason you need to praise them for the effort and not intelligence is that they aren't always going to be successful in the first attempt at things. They may get the first job they interview for, but it isn't always a guarantee. They may fall in love at first sight, but it may not last a lifetime. If the recent pandemic has taught us anything at all, it is this: Life is going to be unpredictable. One day, you are sitting with your legs up on the desk, and the next day, you come to find out that your company went bankrupt. Similarly, children are going to experience some unfortunate events in their lives. However, how prepared they are to deal with them and plan a counter-action is what matters. This is only possible when they are praised for who they are and not what they have achieved. It is about making the effort to do something.

There is a saying by G. K. Chesterton goes like this: "If a thing is worth doing, it's worth doing badly" (Goodreads, n.d.). Many might not make sense of it because we have always been told to try and achieve perfection in everything. We have been told that we shouldn't do something if we aren't good at it. However, G. K. Chesterton is a man who has his name on 80 books, 4,000 essays, and over 200 short stories— he surely knows better. According to him, we must do things poorly, half-heartedly, or as they say, half-assed. The idea is to take action. After all, isn't it better to walk 200 steps a day instead of 2,000 steps? Isn't it better to write 200 words than commit to 2,500 words and never make it past that? Isn't it better to brush your teeth for 30 seconds than not at all?

Poorly doing things still involves taking some form of action than sitting back and waiting for some miracle to happen and do everything as planned. Doing things poorly is always better than doing nothing, and that is a principle your young one should live by. So what if their efforts don't garner results today? A plant takes years before it starts to grow fruit. Taking small steps over a long course is better than doing nothing at all. When you develop the habit of taking action, you won't have to rely on your luck to take you forward in your pursuits. You will learn to rely on your actions and willingness to change. You will rely on your abilities and skills to take you closer to your set goals. You won't have to worry about falling behind because you will still be better off than never starting.

Making Effort Is Equally Important

When a child fails at something, say they get a bad grade, doesn't get on to the sports team, doesn't hear from the college they had been waiting to go to, or gets dumped before the prom by their partner, it's easy to lose heart.

"But I did my best in the test, Mom. Why didn't Miss Jones grade me higher?"

"She was my everything. How will I ever get over her?"

"But I have been practicing for over a year now—every day for two hours straight. How can the coach bench me?"

These are all examples that show how discouraged a child feels. Since disappointments and heartbreaks are part of life, we need to teach children to get over them with resilience and confidence. We need to encourage them to keep trying, giving their best shot, and not lose heart. If the heartbreak or failure is a recent development, chances are they are not going to be open about all the advice and lecture. So how about not relying on it and making them see the bright side of things in some other interesting ways? Take a look at these activities and exercises to help an otherwise discouraged child to reinstate their confidence in their abilities and talents.

What Are My Goals?

Goal setting is a great way to help children stick with their future long-term plans and make progress. Helping them set goals also prevents failures and setbacks, as they can be anticipated, and alternative plans can be set in motion. If we notice, discouragement occurs when a child fails to live up to the expectations we have set for them, but what are expectations if not goals? To make expectations align with reality, they have to be realistic and achievable. Otherwise, a mistake or failure is bound to happen. Therefore, the first activity looks at how parents can help children set short-term and long-term goals.

Having set expectations and goals in motion, children can give their best shot and stay on track. There are many ways to plan this out with them. You can create a chart, a spreadsheet, or even a goals ladder where you and your child list their top goals and how you two plan to achieve them. Once the goals are set, you can talk about expectations such as, "I want you to study at least an hour or practice the violin for at least 20 minutes a day." You can also set expectations regarding routines and chores in the house. The clearer you are, the better.

Here's the Silver Lining

When parents fail to offer the right amount of praise for their effort, children become afraid of failure. They become cautious of their steps to avoid making a mistake and therefore fail to explore creative and innovative ways to do something. Here's what you are going to do. Whenever you find them discouraged because they failed at something, sit down with them and talk about what went wrong—without judgment or sarcasm. Get into the details of what went wrong and try to look at the situation from a positive angle. So what if they failed to score the highest marks in a test? Just look at how much they have learned about new things. Talk about your own mistakes and failures and share the tips that helped you overcome them. Let them not be afraid of making a mistake. Let them see failure as education and not a setback.

Revisit the Past

When a child feels stuck and unwilling to take further action, remind them of their precious moments of disappointments and how they overcame them. It could be a difficult puzzle, learning a new language, solving math problems, or giving a speech in class. Emphasize how proud you were when they finally had the guts to stand strong, take action, and not fear the results. Doing so will boost their confidence and remind them that they can achieve anything they want to in life. It will also tell them that they have it within them to overcome any obstacle they come across. They just need to be creative and keep trying.

You can also make it a weekly family session where you highlight something amazing they did, no matter how insignificant, so that they can feel confident in their abilities.

Chapter 3:

Set High but Realistic

Expectations

The term "expectation" has a negative connotation. It comes with a premeditated idea that something unrealistic is anticipated in return. However, this isn't always the case. When we set expectations for our children, we become strict and rigid. We want them to be disciplined and obedient. We want them to be raised as perfect individuals without a flaw in sight. However, this strictness prevents elasticity that is important for their growth and mental peace. If they constantly feel like they have to prove their worth, be on their best behavior, and follow all the rules by the book, they can never be themselves. They can't be expressive of their creativity because a certain level of obedience is expected of them. This also limits their thinking and makes them followers in a herd and not the leader.

True, expectations should direct children's behaviors, aspirations, self-esteem, and enthusiasm, but they shouldn't become a parameter against which we judge them. They should help children prosper—not put them down.

Since the goal is to promote critical thinking and raise an adult that is confident about their opinions and can see through the double-meaning agendas of people and media, we need to reassess the expectations we have from them. Expectations should help them outline what is anticipated of them and serve as a manual. For example, if you want your child to behave well in a social gathering, they should know what is ultimately expected of them and what will happen if they don't truly fulfill those expectations. This doesn't always have to be a threatening suggestion but rather one that helps them stay disciplined.

Expectations also ensure safety. A child that knows that they shouldn't run on the roads or engage in drugs and substance abuse will remain distant from such activities because they know of the expectations their parents have for them.

On the other hand, a child may be informed of the expectations of their school grades and the educational levels their parents expect from them.

Expectations: High or Low?

Claudia Alta, aka "Lady Bird Johnson," a first lady of the United States of America, once said that children live up to the expectations we expect of them; there has been some solid evidence proposing that parental involvement and beliefs largely influence a child's success or failure rate (Damon et al., 2006). Studies show that when expectations set by the parents are great, children are likely to live up to them. The expectations we set for our children play a key role in determining their social and academic outcomes.

According to a 2000 survey by the National Center on Addiction and Substance Abuse (CASA), researchers studied two different modes of parenting: hands-off and hands-on parenting. Hands-off families were those where the parents played a passive role in the child's upbringing or had little to no expectations from the child. In such households, the children are free to pick what they like to do and how they like to do it. In hands-on families, parents monitored a child's activities and had expectations from them. These included participating in dinner conversations, being obedient, following routines, and doing their best at school. During the survey, researchers analyzed a few thousand teenagers and monitored their attitudes and behaviors. They found that teenagers raised in households where the parents set expectations and took an interest in their child's lives were less likely to turn to self-damaging behaviors like engaging in drugs or being rude toward their parents or siblings ("'Hands-On' Parents Help Teens Say No to Drugs,'" 2001).

However, when we say to "have great expectations," is it synonymous with "high"?

Some studies endorse the idea of setting high expectations from children. They believe that by doing so, children are more likely to do well in school and career (Hossler & Stage, 1992). The same study also suggests that these kids are less likely to drop out of school. Another study revealed that parent's expectations have a strong influence on the type of relationships a child has with its peers and partners (Burks & Parke, 1996).

Another study found that when parents, especially the mother, hold high expectations from their child, the child is likely to perform at their best (Benner & Mistry, 2007). The study compared the impact between an expectation set by a mother and an educator. The children studied belonged to poor urban households, aged between 9 all the way to 16. The study found that the child performed at their best when both the educator and the mother held high expectations. However, the mother's expectations had a buffering effect on the occasions when the teacher's expectations turned low, meaning when the child knew that their mother had faith in their abilities, the child experienced positive academic outcomes. This wasn't the case when the roles were reversed, and the educator had high hopes from the child and the mother didn't.

This further stresses the important role parents have to play in raising a thinker. A child's loyalty is toward their parents first. It is heartbreaking for them to let down their parents. Therefore, be a parent that sets high expectations for their children. These high expectations, however, must be just and realistic.

But how high should the expectations be?

In one study, researchers aimed to look at the impact of parental over-aspiration in students from Germany and the United States (Murayama et al., 2016). The findings revealed that when parents had unreasonable expectations from their children, it didn't have the desired effect. Instead of overachieving, the child's performance declined over the year. This suggests that expectations shouldn't be too high or unrealistic because it can lead to one failure after another, damaging a child's confidence in their abilities. The repeated disappointment also resulted in the children giving up on their curiosity and doing things differently. The goal changed from learning and exploration to cramming and staying within the comfort zones. Besides, every child is different and therefore deserves a different set of expectations. In short, the expectations should align with the interests and abilities of the child. Also, the parents must stay engaged and track the progress the child is making to ensure that they aren't being too harsh.

Be Compassionate: Don't Turn Into a Taskmaster

Every child is unique, and they have different learning paces. Your eldest might have started walking before they turned one. This doesn't mean your youngest will do the same. Likewise, your eldest might show more interest in studying while your youngest spends most of their time playing games or watching YouTube. They are both different, unique, and equally precious. As a parent, you must have different strategies to handle their tantrums and misbehaviors. You might have to calmly tell your eldest to spend some time outdoors whereas you might have to physically drag your youngest away from the TV so that they can spend an hour finishing up their homework.

When it comes to setting expectations for both, you have to show compassion and kindness. You can't expect them both to be sporty and nerdy at the same time. You can't expect them both to react to the daily happenings and problems in the same manner.

As they both pick up things at different paces and have different perspectives of viewing the world, the expectations you set for both of them have to be different too.

Encourage critical thinking and intelligence by setting the right expectations, but don't act like a taskmaster. Show some leniency; sit down and talk about what you expect of them and notice the effort they put in to reach those expectations. For example, if one child fails to do well in a test while the other aces it, don't treat the first child like an outcast. Maybe you expected too much of them, and they failed to live up to those expectations. In that case, re-evaluate and lower your expectations to some extent so as not to discourage learning and critical thinking. If a child repeatedly fails to live up to the set expectations of their parents, they will lose their confidence and stop trying. Learning or practicing something won't interest them because they would view themselves as a failure. They would prefer not doing something than to be labeled a failure again.

Setting Realistic Expectations for Children

A child gains confidence when they complete a task. However, that task has to be something that resonates with their abilities and talents. You can't judge them for being poor keyboard players when they have never taken a single lesson. When it comes to setting expectations, the goal should be to gradually increase them (Wright et al., 1995). Think of it as playing a more difficult level. The game remains the same, but there are just more obstacles. That is how you can encourage a positive mindset as well as boost learning. When a child feels challenged, they are more likely to try harder. They will come up with new ways of attempting things in the assigned time. Make the task slightly more difficult but not too difficult, as it will scare them off. Martin Seligman believes that too much failure can result in learned helplessness (Ackerman, 2021b).

So how can you encourage taking action, boost learning, and raise a thinker by setting the right expectations? Here are some ideas:

Let Me In

When children have a say in what is expected of them, they are more likely to then live up to them. Whenever setting new rules in place, be sure to include them—especially if they directly impact them. For example, if you expect them to take up more responsibility in the house, ask them what chores they would like to stick with. Having the chance to pick and choose can foster responsibility. The same applies to other important matters such as getting into a good college, getting a job, or moving out. If a child feels that their opinion on the matter is valued and validated, they will be more encouraged to put forth their best work.

Vision Board

A vision board is another fun and entertaining way to encourage goal setting as well as setting the right expectations. This is an activity that both the parent and the child can take part in. You simply start with some old newspapers and magazines and cut out pictures that resonate with a goal you have in mind. For example, if the goal is to become a lawyer, your vision board can have pictures of successful lawyers your child looks up to, motivational quotes to help them get there, and any small steps that they need to take in that regard. For example, getting into a good law school can be a great start. You can add a cutout of one of the finest and top-rated law schools in the country.

The idea is to help your child visualize and keep a track of what they want in life. Every time they revisit the vision board, they will be reminded of the goal and become motivated. As for the parents, you can help them actualize that goal by setting expectations such as getting good grades in school, being on their best behavior, being responsible, etc.

Expectation Charts

Similar to creating a vision board, expectation charts help parents track and monitor their child's behavior and effort. An expectation chart should list all the expectations that you have from your child—given that they are achievable and realistic. You can also have a big expectation divided into smaller goals and objectives—expanded over weeks or months. For example, if they are a teenager and deliberately putting off finding a decent place to work, make an expectation chart with the amount of time they have to find a job. Once they do, you can create another expectation chart that lists how much they are supposed to contribute to the household if they plan to stay. Then, using a similar chart, you can help them move out, find a place of their own, and start paying bills using their money.

Chapter 4:

Cultivate a Growth Mindset

To promote creative thinking, one has to have a growth mindset. Learning is a process that encompasses hard work, patience, and failure. Without hard work, there are no positive rewards. Without patience, one can never become resilient. Without failure, there is little innovation. There are over 100 examples of famous experiments that went wrong. Some ended with creating new and important innovations, whereas others focused on improving the design of an existing idea. Who would have thought a few centuries ago that we would now be able to transmit data within milliseconds across continents or circle the world in a few days?

Who would have thought that an eagerness to fly in the skies would lead two brothers to come up with the idea of an airplane? They didn't succeed the first time, did they? Yet they remained determined. There was also some delay due to persistently poor weather and technical issues, yet they remained patient. They failed several times before they successfully flew for 59 seconds and covered a distance of 852 feet ("The Wright Flyer: From Invention to Icon," n.d.).

Many similar stories attest to the power of a positive mindset and one that knows no fear. Such a mindset is a growth mindset where an individual strongly believes that they can improve and master any skill and talent if they try hard enough.

A growth mindset is essential to raise a thinker. A growth mindset urges a child to retain their curiosity by doing things differently. They are made to step out of their comfort zone and be creative. They handle hardships and difficulties by facing their fears. They view failures and mistakes as opportunities for growth instead of setbacks. They don't feel like a failure when they don't become an expert at something after trying it once. They believe in perseverance and patience.

On the other hand, children with a fixed mindset believe that they are born with all the qualities and traits they will ever master. Their thinking and creativity are limited by their thoughts. They are reluctant to try new things or methods and have self-esteem issues. They find it hard to take in criticism and work on themselves. They would rather surrender than try another time. Since they stick to old methods of doing things and can't think outside the box, they find fewer growth opportunities. According to researchers Peter Heslin, Don Vandewalle, and Gary Latham, managers with a fixed mindset are less likely to take in advice from others or welcome feedback from employees with a growth mindset (Heslin et al., 2006). Unlike managers with a growth mindset, they don't view themselves as work in progress and fail to take in constructive criticism well. They feel like being told where to improve is a direct reflection of how poor they are at work. They instantly start to doubt their competence.

The same is true for children. Children with a fixed mindset are quick to give up instead of working on themselves. This doesn't promote a positive mindset because the child is constantly surrounded by negative thoughts about themselves. They believe that they don't have it in them to change and turn over a new leaf. They are less likely to seek help and assistance from others, as it makes them feel incompetent. Conversely, a child with a growth mindset not only thinks differently but is also quick to seek any form of assistance. They are open to being coached and guided when they lose track.

To say that your mindset affects the quality of your actions, relationships, and success won't be wrong. A positive mindset makes one remain inquisitive. This is one reason why, as parents, we must encourage curiosity and exploration. How else would they learn to think for themselves if they don't interact with others, don't actively question things, or explore new avenues?

Encourage Exploration

Exploration is one of the reasons for the most profound discoveries and amazing revelations. From scientists to medical experts or from astronomers to authors who weave a fantasy world straight out of their minds, exploration has led us to many otherwise unimaginable findings. From the search for natural resources to finding new trade routes or from curious explorers finding sources of life on inhabitable planets to finding new species in the depths of waters, there is always something new to learn about. This exploratory drive is a human trait and has been one of the driving forces behind every invention we have today. A child learns to use their hand-eye coordination to pick up things. It is their curiosity that further motivates them to roll over, crawl, and then walk. It is the same driving force that makes them want to know everything about the world as they begin to speak. Then, they find something unique about themselves and hone that talent to the fullest. Every step of the way, we have been inspired by our need to explore and discover something new.

Several studies believe that children learn best when they are driven by their curiosity. Why is the sky blue and the water colorless? Why do we ride some animals but not all? Why can fish swim and monkeys climb on trees? These are all questions that lead to many discoveries about how things work and what can be done to improve that. It also cultivates the search for something better. If you want to take a look at how far curiosity has led us, just look around yourself. Look at the light in your room, the air conditioner throwing in cool air, the stove cooking your food, and the TV broadcasting amazing shows. Using curiosity as a means of learning, children can craft their thinking. Below are some reasons why you should encourage exploration.

Exploration-based learning helps young minds develop a sense of self, as they can immerse themselves in investigative subjects, objects, and scenarios that interest them. Exploration-based learning is self-guided learning. Allowing a child to learn by permitting them to pick their interests and explore them in an educational setting encourages them to become independent and autonomous. With some instructions and resources from parents, children can quench their thirst for knowledge in a way that suits them best. Also, there is evidence that suggests that visual learning is better than any other form of learning. Exploration-based learning is mostly visually aided learning, making the overall concept of learning interesting.

When children have the free will to learn as they like, it puts the responsibility on them. Parents or educators are no longer the only ones responsible for educating the child. Their curiosity serves as guidance. They are more driven and inspired. They ask more genuine and thought-provoking questions, thus becoming a critical thinker. When they seek assistance either from their teachers, friends, or parents, they actively engage in social conversations which also build their confidence. They develop the ability to mold their questions to become productive. When they find something they are interested in, they are more likely to cultivate a goal-oriented attitude. The ability to converse, cooperate, accept others' opinions, and have a goal-oriented mindset are all essential skills that employers seek in potential candidates. This means that children with a growth mindset and exploratory skills have better prospects when it comes to landing a job of their liking.

Speaking of collaboration and increased social interactions, self-guided, exploration-based learning also helps children learn to respect the boundaries of others and themselves. They can acquire valuable traits like empathy, acceptance, and teamwork. They can find people with the same interests as themselves and further enhance their understanding of a topic or thing. This will make learning collaborative. The more minds that are engaged, the better the comprehension. Each individual can help out the other in gaining a new and deeper perspective. It's like two fans of Marvel. From watching all the movies, reading the comics, to collecting their favorite Marvel action figures, they can create a world of their own and many spin-off stories. Sadly, traditional lecture-style classrooms don't offer such exploration and engagement.

Finally, encouraging children to explore can help them discover their true interests, passions, and talents. Discovery is usually bound to a means of creative expression like theater, music, or dancing. Passions can involve mastering a talent or interest and gaining more knowledge about it. Talents involve getting to know what makes you unique and that is only possible when the child feels motivated to try and explore new things.

Encourage Risk-Taking and Problem-Solving

Risk-taking doesn't mean that you push the child into the unknown. Risk-taking involves facing challenges and hardships one would otherwise not face. Healthy risk-taking is a lot like exploration. You allow the child to tap into an unknown potential and hope that they come out as a victor. Healthy risk-taking along with building problem-solving skills prepares children to independently face difficult times and problems. While it may be natural for you to want to keep your child safe from any form of injury, you shouldn't forget that injuries are also a learning experience. In exchange for the physical and emotional pain that they go through, they also learn how to be safe.

Parents who stop their children from healthy risk-taking raise insecure and unconfident children. These children seek validation from others for everything they do. They require permission and some pushing when it comes to expecting them to do something alone. But since the goal is to develop a growth mindset, exploration, healthy risk-taking, and problem-solving skills are all a necessity if you want your children to wander independently, be confident about their skills and abilities, and encounter setbacks with grit. Here are some strategies to help them take health risks and develop problem-solving skills:

Attempt the Impossible

This can be a great weekly or monthly exercise for you and your little one. This can help you form a stronger bond with them, keep a track of their progress, offer support, and help them develop confidence. You start with a goal that has always been on your checklist but never got done. It can be taking up a new habit, following a childhood passion, or doing something that takes guts and courage. The idea is to commit to working on that goal and being accountable for it. You both should set a goal and attempt to pull it off. The harder the goal, the more the satisfaction of completing it. This exercise encourages children to step out of their comfort zones and take healthy risks.

At the end of the week, talk about the progress you made, discuss how you could have achieved the goal differently, and how you plan to stick to what you have learned. Then, it will be time for another goal-setting exercise.

Encourage Initiation

Whenever you are at a restaurant, shopping mall, or grocery store, encourage young children to take the initiative of ordering food, paying the bill at the counter, or emptying the cart at the cashier. Having the chance to do something that most elders do will encourage risk-taking and accountability. These interactions will make them more confident, vocal about their opinions and demands, and interactive.

Set Up an Interview

Ask your child to interview someone they view as inspirational or courageous. Set up an interview and help them draft the questions they would want the interviewee to answer. Emphasize discussing the methods that worked for them when they faced a setback or loss. Hearing about someone's personal stories of how they overcame failures and losses is a great way to teach young children about persistence, problem-solving, and healthy risk-taking. The more intrigued and inspired they are, the more likely they will follow through with the advice they received.

Chapter 5:

Build Resilience

Resilience is the power to bounce back from adversities. Some have no choice but to move on while others can do so. The difference lies in the willingness. Naturally resilient children are quick to get over failures and losses. When life pulls them down, they get up, brush the dust off, and are on their way once again. Children who lack resilience and grit aren't able to do so. They rely on others to come and get them because one failure becomes the definition of who they are.

Building strong and resilient skills also promotes thinking. What comes after a setback is the need for a different approach. To be creative, you need to concoct new methods. This is impossible without good thinking skills. How can you expect a child to not repeat the same mistakes if they don't ponder over the first one enough?

Besides, resilience has many other benefits, too. Being resilient allows children to deal with their matters autonomously. Be it bullying, racial abuses, or any form of trauma, resilient children can overcome it all with their grit and confidence. Since resilience isn't a fixed trait, every parent has the chance to foster it in young minds. Flexibility, perseverance, and adaptability are all distinctive features of resilience and allow children to tap into themselves and their thoughts.

Developing resilience in children can be both complex and personal. Building resilience involves getting to know your inner strengths, an estimate of your outer resources, and a willingness to become better and improved. What differentiates resilient thinkers and non-resilient thinkers is that resilient thinkers have an action-oriented approach. They don't give up easily, their wounds heal faster, and their minds work faster and in creative ways.

Raise a Resilient Thinker

Resilience gives people the emotional strength and a positive mindset to cope with hardships, adversity, and trauma. Resilient children can utilize this strength to overcome challenges and handle setbacks. Non-resilient thinkers feel helpless and overwhelmed when faced with a crisis. They have unhealthy coping mechanisms that lead to several mental health issues like stress, increased anxiety, and depression. According to one study, patients who attempted suicide had lower resilience scores than patients who never attempted it (Fletcher & Sarkar, 2013). This is just an indicator of how insecure non-resilient thinkers can be.

Certainly, you wouldn't want to raise an adult who isn't able to cope with the daily stresses of life. Below are qualities that you would want to see and hone in your child:

1. **Acceptance:** Resilient thinkers accept things as they are. They process each passing moment in real time with real facts. They don't let their emotions get the best of them because their thoughts are positive and realistic.

2. **Compromise:** Resilient thinkers have an "adjust as you go" mentality. They believe in staying flexible—both in body and mind. They address only the immediate needs and then move on.

3. **Connection:** Resilient thinkers stay connected with their educators, peers, and parents. They understand that to think great, they need different opinions and ideas. Staying connected also offers them the support and motivation they need to keep moving forward.

4. **Excellent Coping Skills:** Coping skills are important in facing adversities. Having healthy coping mechanisms is another quality of resilient thinkers. They rely on skills like meditation, spiritual connection, therapy, mindfulness, and writing to cope with their emotions.

Mistakes Aren't Always a Bad Thing

Bouncing back with improved confidence and increased dedication isn't something everyone has the power to do. Sometimes, this power has to be fed into the minds through genuine support, validation of emotions, and encouragement. This is especially true when a child commits a mistake. This is where the role of parents comes in. Since a child trusts them the most, they are naturally inclined to hear what they have to offer. In a case where a mistake or setback has occurred, the right words and appreciation matter a lot. Therefore, acceptance and bouncing back are possible when the child feels supported and guided. Below are some exercises and activities that offer advice on how to build resilience in children after they have made a mistake and help them view it as a learning lesson as opposed to a setback.

Let's Find a Purpose

Finding something that makes you happy is an instant happiness booster. A meaningful purpose adds happiness and improves one's emotional and mental state. To build resilience, help your child find a purpose they are genuinely interested in. This way, even when they face a setback, they will keep going because they are driven by the rewards and satisfaction it guarantees. For example, if a child is interested in playing an instrument, a few setbacks like not getting the model they wanted, unavailability of a mentor, or lack of time won't discourage them. If anything, they will think of ways to overcome those setbacks using productive means. To help them find that purpose, below are a few questions you can ask them:

- What is the one thing you truly can't live without?

- What is the first thing you want to do when you get up every morning?

- What do you dream about?

- What thoughts keep you awake at night?

- What activity makes you feel alive?

- How would you define success in any area of your life?

- If you were asked to sum up your ultimate goal in life, how would you define it?

When Was the Last Time I Was Resilient?

Children make mistakes all the time. They don't realize how quickly they make amends unless they are reminded. Use reminders about an experience where your child overcame the setbacks they faced. Go into the details of how much courage they had shown and how proud you were of them. Be sure to emphasize how creatively they thought and changed their perspectives and methods. Also, remind them how great they felt after they overcame the challenging time. This should renew some faith in their ability to overcome adversities and motivate them to try harder again.

It Could Have Been Worse

This final exercise is an excellent way to brighten up an otherwise depressed and sad child. The activity involves some thinking as to what could have happened. It could be worse allowing children to think of a situation differently—given it was worse. For example, if they are depressed because they fought with their best friend, ask them to imagine a world where they had no friends to talk to or no family to look after them. Ask them to visualize how a life without friends or family would look and how it would make them feel.

Imagining a situation in this manner takes away the focus from the core of it. Instead, the child begins to see how things could have turned out worse and appreciate what they have.

Chapter 6:

Answer Their "Whys"

I understand how annoying it can get when your child keeps asking you questions about the most random things. It irks us, and there comes a point when we decide to shut them down by engaging them in some other activity. I like to call this the "parental blunder." It's a blunder because not only are you taking away the chance to increase their knowledge, but you are also telling them that being curious isn't a good thing. Why? Well, it upsets Mommy and Daddy, and they'll get scolded!

Retaining curiosity as a child gets older is one of the most amazing gifts in life. We tend to stop asking questions because we think it bothers others. Has it ever happened to you in class where you had multiple questions to ask from your teacher but decided not to because the whole class seemed to be against you? You know you hated that kid, too. They would make the lecture longer because of their inquisitive mind.

Asking questions is how the world becomes predictable for children. They learn through experiences and questions. The brain works best when it predicts well. Many parents make the mistake of asking "why" questions with answers like, "Because I said so." This does not explain anything and discourages the child. If there is something you want them to abstain from, tell them why they should instead of scaring them off. For example, if you want them to not eat more than two cookies at a time, tell them why you don't allow it. Talk about the hazards of consuming too much sugar. Talk about the dangers of gaining weight and how it can hinder their everyday activities. That is how you break a bad habit—not by scolding a child. Offering age-appropriate reasoning can keep the curiosity alive and make them excellent thinkers.

Look for Teachable Moments

What is a teachable moment? A teachable moment is one where a child's development happens the fastest. The best part is that they don't even know that they are being taught something. A child is most receptive when they can learn something in a lecture-free manner. They seem more receptive to everyday conversations than when you sit down with them for homework. A teachable moment is instantaneous. It can happen once a day or several times. For example, if you begin watching a movie with your children, this could be a teachable moment where you talk about the feelings or situations the main character is in and discuss the best strategies to get out of it. Similarly, if you are watching the news with them and news about a tsunami is being broadcasted, it can be a great moment to talk to them about the various forces of nature and tsunamis in the past as well as the destruction they caused.

All you need is to pay attention and stay vigilant. A teachable moment can occur in the form of an innocent question from your child about why bears live in the forest or why beavers build homes over water. You then have an opportunity to pique their interest in the ways animals live, what they eat, and how they survive in the wild. In case you don't know the answers to all of their questions, encourage researching about it online. Thanks to search engines, you can have millions of results showcased in a fraction of a second. You can find the answers and discuss them with your child.

You can also try DIY teachable moments. For instance, if you find them reading a book, you can ask them about the story, the struggles of the main character, how they overcome those struggles, and their courageous attitude—these are all great topics to discuss and teach them about.

You can also ask them to craft, do chores or groceries, and introduce them to the many things you use in the house daily. You can engage them in stories from your past. For example, if you are making toast in a toaster, you can talk about life before you had a toaster in your house and how you used to have toast then.

To encourage a talk about money matters, you can take them to the bank with you or help them devise a weekly budget. You can even discuss any newsworthy stories or commercials that you see on TV.

Always Be Present and Creative

Being present, engaged, and interested in your children's activities and actions is a great way to stay connected. You get the chance to spot many teachable moments and bond with them by asking open-ended questions that promote curiosity. I have compiled three strategies below to help foster curiosity in children at every age:

Let's Try This Today

Research some of the most sought-after qualities and skills that your children can take advantage of when they become adults. Many parents believe that children should be encouraged to do what they like. This is true, but a slight nudge in the right direction can make them excel in things other children aren't competent at. For example, if they are a teenager, encouraging them to pick up additional courses in subjects like computer, math, or home economics can prepare them to tap into whatever field they like. For example, some basic and advanced courses in computers about web and graphic designing, software, app development, etc. can help them earn some side money if they have any kind of free time on their hands. They may even apply for jobs in industries they would have a hard time entering otherwise, like entertainment and tech companies.

Get them excited about a new activity every few months and encourage them to take it.

Give Them the Means to Outshine and Master

Your work is only halfway done. You also need to provide them the means to excel in the activities they choose. For instance, if they want to tap into the gaming world by learning animation and making basic games on Android, look up some courses or mentors that would help them achieve their goal. Thanks to many free websites like YouTube, they can find the related material easily and get started.

Reimagine Famous Worlds

What if there was a crossover between the *Harry Potter* characters and the *Lord of the Rings* characters? How would have Harry destroyed the ring using magic or Frodo fought Voldemort? Reimagine famous stories to pique creativity and curiosity. Give your child everyday scenarios and ask them to think about them differently. For instance, how would Daddy do the laundry or how would Mommy wash the car? Such open-ended and thought-provoking questions can give their curiosity muscles some much-needed exercise. Such activities can help them come up with new ways of thinking, viewing things from a different perspective, and generate new ideas—all promoting thinking in its essence.

Chapter 7:

Provide a Healthy

Environment for Growth

Some parents are carpenters; some are gardeners. Carpenters carve wood into a shape they desire whereas a gardener helps plants grow. They both start with nothing and end up with a valuable product. Being a carpenter parent means that you sculpt the child into something specific. A gardener parent simply offers a healthy environment for the plant to grow in. The plant can take whatever form it desires.

It isn't wrong of you to desire the best for your child. You are hard on them because you want only the best things in life to come to them. You want to see them prosper and succeed in all areas of life, but this doesn't mean that you have to force them into doing the things you want them to do. Many parents realize later how their poor choices and intervention in their child's life has raised them as an unhappy adult. They get into a career they hate.

The ideal goal should be to offer them a healthy and supportive family and space to grow up in. You can still be hard and strict with the rules, provided that you let them who they want to be. This means that you allow them to seek a passion or career and then help them succeed in it by offering moral and emotional support. As a gardener, you must first know what type of plant you are growing and then adjust the soil and nutrients accordingly.

What Does a Healthy Environment Look Like?

A healthy environment for growth is one where the child feels important and validated. All their basic needs are met. They feel loved and valued. They feel supported and safe. They know that they can openly discuss important issues with their parents and siblings and engage in healthy arguments. There is acceptance and empathy. There is kindness and affection. There is no prejudice or competition. Each child is loved equally and often. Such a home is essential to raise a healthy and happy adult.

A lot of this relies on the type of relationships a child has with the parent. In a busy world like ours where many parents work full-time jobs, it can be difficult to give children the time and attention they deserve. From store-bought meals to staying occupied at work, our busy schedules make our children feel unloved. They have no one to talk to, communicate about their day's activities, or help with homework.

Therefore, the first step in fostering a healthy and growth-oriented environment at home begins with increasing the amount of time spent together. This doesn't mean having dinner alone. It involves taking out the time to spend with the kids and talking about something new and interesting. The idea is to remain connected so that the child feels supported. When they see their parents happily engaged with them, not only does it make them happy, but it also boosts their confidence. They feel comfortable talking about subjects that are of importance and let their parents have a say in it. This encourages the generation of more ideas and perspectives—helping both parents and children bond with one another.

Apart from healthy interactions, some other important features of a healthy and safe environment include the following:

1. **Emotional Support:** In a healthy home, a child never feels left out emotionally. Their feelings and emotions are validated. There is active listening involved that is free of judgment and lecturing. Effective communication is at play that allows all family members to reach a consensus that is in the best interest of everyone. Issues are resolved without the need for shouting or yelling out instructions. Healthy

coping mechanisms are utilized to deal with any stresses and hardships.

2. **Focus On Healthy Nutrition:** There is also a strong emphasis on eating healthy. In healthy homes, meals are cooked with love using fresh ingredients for the most benefits. There is an abundance of grains, lentils, green vegetables, and healthy proteins that offer a boost of energy.

3. **Exercise and Outdoor Activities:** Parents in a healthy home offer children ample opportunities for exercise and outdoor play. From gardening and car washing to building a treehouse with all the children from the neighborhood, many fun activities keep the children engaged in healthy movement.

4. **Routines:** There are some strict routines about technology usage in the house. There are parental checks on phones and TV that prevent the corruption of young minds. Family-oriented programs are watched as a family and followed by healthy discussions. There are also fixed bedtimes to allow children to get high-quality sleep every night.

5. **Responsibilities:** Children are given chores and responsibilities in a healthy environment.

Parents understand that learning important life skills is essential for their growth and future success. These tasks teach children about taking ownership and mastering them. The completion is then praised with applause and rewards.

Read to Them... A Lot

The kind of activities a child is exposed to from an early age also determines the type of individual they will be. In earlier times, women were taught to stay at home, learn how to sew, cook, and please their husbands. The men were taught how to work, earn money, and find the perfect woman. Luckily, we have come out of that era and afforded our children with more valuable and creative skills and activities. When we talk about creating a healthy environment for growth, we can't exclude reading as an essential activity.

To raise a leader and critical thinker, stress must be made on reading books. It is the best form of exploration and learning. Since children learn from the influences around them, you have to become an avid reader and promote the habit of reading in your house. Evidence points out that children start to pick up words and their meanings when they are just a few months old. This means that even if you think that they don't understand what you are reading to them, they do (Perszyk & Waxman, 2018).

This builds neural connections that help in learning. The more words they are exposed to, the greater the effect. Unlike their peers, their reading comprehension will improve, and they will have better vocabulary. Since reading stimulates the brain and introduces different worlds to us, it should be requisite in healthy homes. Books should be made accessible to young children so that they can model good reading habits. To encourage this healthy habit, I have a set of tips for you.

1. **Read From Day One:** No matter how little they are or naive they seem, children see and hear everything: It is how they learn about the world around them. Therefore, start a reading routine and continue until they are old enough to read a book themselves.

2. **Search Local Libraries and Make Sure to Visit Them Now and Then:** You can have your child get their library card made and have the choice to pick one book every week to read. You can start with simple short stories and notice what themes and genres interest your child the most. Later, you can help them pick the best stories and informational books in those niches.

3. **Reread Your Favorite Books and Stories:** When children are young, they love to hear their favorite tales over and over again. Rereading books can help them hear or

comprehend something they missed the first time.

4. **If They Enjoy Reading a Particular Author, Make it Accessible to Them:** Purchase it for them for a job well done or surprise them with a set on special occasions like birthdays and Christmas.

5. **Create a Dedicated Reading Station With a Shelf Filled With Your Child's Favorite Books:** Make sure to keep that area as free of distractions as possible so that the child can truly immerse themselves in reading. Having a dedicated area to themselves will further motivate them to read.

6. **To Raise a Thinker, Don't Just Limit Your Child's Reading to Books and Novels:** Make use of technology, media, magazines, and other nonfiction reads as well. The more options they have, the better. For example, if a child loves to talk about turtles, introduce them to the many news articles, kids encyclopedias, and posters based on them.

Conclusion

Critical thinkers can tell facts from fantasy. They can see through the biases and prejudice. They can differentiate between right and wrong. They are born leaders—not followers. They know how to get their word across. They are considerate, have healthy boundaries, love to explore, and nurture their curiosity. They are driven by a passion for learning about anything and everything. They are responsible and sensible. They have healthy coping mechanisms to deal with the daily stresses of life. They are resilient and have faith in their abilities and talents. They know that if they try hard enough, they can conquer anything. They are resilient and unafraid of uncertainty. They are empathic and compassionate. They can have model conversations and form positive social connections.

By the looks of it, it seems like they are an ideal individual destined to succeed in life with the right set of social and life skills.

Luckily, all these skills can be built in young minds with a little help. Support and motivation by the parents in the form of a healthy and prospering environment to grow in along with healthy reading habits can help children retain their inquisitiveness and not settle for third-party answers. They can form opinions of their own and rely on their sound judgment to make important life decisions.

It is you who can raise them to be a thinker. You now have the tools to hone good habits in them from early on and encourage a positive mindset that promises a good life at the end of the day.

Thank you for giving this book a read. I hope you loved reading it as much as I enjoyed writing it. It would make me the happiest person on earth if you would take a moment to leave an honest review. All you have to do is visit the site where you purchased this book: It's that simple! The review doesn't have to be a full-fledged paragraph; a few words will do. Your few words will help others decide if this is what they should be reading as well. Thank you in advance, and best of luck with your parenting adventures. Every moment is a joyous one with a child.

References

Ackerman, C. E. (2021a). *27 resilience activities and worksheets for students and adults (+pdfs)*. PositivePsychology.com. https://positivepsychology.com/resilience-activities-worksheets/

Ackerman, C. E. (2021b). *Learned Helplessness: Seligman's Theory of Depression (+ Cure)*. Positive Psychology.com. https://positivepsychology.com/learned-helplessness-seligman-theory-depression-cure/

Benner, A. D., & Mistry, R. S. (2007). Congruence of mother and teacher educational expectations and low-income youth's academic competence. *Journal of Educational Psychology*, *99*(1), 140–153. https://doi.org/10.1037/0022-0663.99.1.140

Burks, V. S., & Parke, R. D. (1996). Parent and child representations of social relationships: Linkages between families and peers. *Merrill-Palmer Quarterly*, *42*(3), 358–378. https://www.jstor.org/stable/23089867

Bursztynsky, J. (2020, August 19). *Apple becomes first U.S. company to reach a $2 trillion market cap.* CNBC. https://www.cnbc.com/2020/08/19/apple-reaches-2-trillion-market-cap.html

Cherry, K. (2019). *How some people are more resilient when it comes to stress.* Verywell Mind. https://www.verywellmind.com/characteristics-of-resilience-2795062

Cherry, K. (2020, June 22). *Influential theories about how children grow and develop.* Verywell Mind. https://www.verywellmind.com/child-development-theories-2795068#piagets-cognitive-developmental-theory

Clements, R. (2014, February 6). *12 things to do when we get discouraged.* Lifehack; Lifehack. https://www.lifehack.org/articles/communication/12-things-when-get-discouraged.html

Co, P. (2017, May 18). *Why kids thrive when we set high expectations.* Parent Co. https://www.parent.com/blogs/conversations/why-our-children-thrive-when-we-set-high-expectations

Courage activities for students & teens: Building risk-taking skills. (n.d.). Growing Leaders. Retrieved

September 21, 2021, from https://growingleaders.com/free-resources/building-courage-and-risk-taking-skills/

Damon, W., Lerner, R. M., & Eisenberg, N. (2006). *Handbook of child psychology.* John Wiley & Sons.

Dewar, G. (2012, January 2). *Teaching critical thinking: An evidence-based guide.* Parenting Science. https://parentingscience.com/teaching-critical-thinking/

Drew, C. (2020, February 1). *What is a teachable moment? - 31 great examples (2021).* Helpfulprofessor.com. https://helpfulprofessor.com/teachable-moment/

Dweck, C. (2015, January 1). *The Secret to Raising Smart Kids.* Scientific American. https://www.scientificamerican.com/article/the-secret-to-raising-smart-kids1/

Fletcher, D., & Sarkar, M. (2013). Psychological resilience: A review and critique of definitions, concepts, and theory. *European Psychologist, 18*(1), 12–23. https://doi.org/10.1027/1016-9040/a000124

4 tips to setting realistic expectations for your child. (2013, September 5). The Confident Mom. https://theconfidentmom.com/09/mom-life/setting-realistic-expectations-for-your-child/

Goodreads. (n.d.). *Quote by G.K. Chesterton.* Goodreads. https://www.goodreads.com/quotes/84521-if-a-thing-is-worth-doing-it-is-worth-doing

Gordon, S. (2021, July 15). *How to Teach Your Child to Be a Critical Thinker.* Verywell Family. https://www.verywellfamily.com/how-to-teach-your-child-to-be-a-critical-thinker-5190765

'Hands-On' Parents Help Teens Say No to Drugs (2001, February 21). *WebMD.* Retrieved September 21, 2021, from http://www.webmd.com/parenting/news/20010221/hands-on-parents-help-teens-say-no-to-drugs#1

Hernstein, R. J., Nickerson, R. S., de Sánchez, M., & Swets, J. A. (1986). Teaching thinking skills. *American Psychologist, 41*(11), 1279–1289. https://doi.org/10.1037/0003-066x.41.11.1279

Heslin, P. A., VandeWalle, D., & Latham, G. P. (2006). Keen to help? Managers' implicit person theories and their subsequent employee coaching. *Personnel Psychology*, *59*(4), 871–902. https://doi.org/10.1111/j.1744-6570.2006.00057.x

Holecko, C. (2021, January 31). *Why risk-taking is healthier than playing it safe*. Verywell Family. https://www.verywellfamily.com/why-risk-taking-is-healthy-for-kids-4118491

Hossler, D., & Stage, F. K. (1992). Family and high school experience influences on the postsecondary educational plans of ninth-grade students. *American Educational Research Journal*, *29*(2), 425–451. https://doi.org/10.3102/00028312029002425

Hurley, K. (2019, November 13). *What is resilience? Definition, types, building resiliency, benefits and resources | everyday health*. EverydayHealth.com. https://www.everydayhealth.com/wellness/resilience/

Mitchell, V. (2017, October 17). *Are you a resilient thinker? Learn 5 steps to become one*. Www.linkedin.com. https://www.linkedin.com/pulse/you-resilient-thinker-learn-5-steps-become-one-veronica-mitchell

Morin, A. (n.d.). *How kids develop thinking and learning skills.* Www.understood.org. https://www.understood.org/articles/en/how-kids-develop-thinking-and-learning-skills

Morin, A. (2019, June 24). *How to take advantage of teachable moments with a child.* Verywell Family. https://www.verywellfamily.com/what-are-teachable-moments-2086537

Murayama, K., Pekrun, R., Suzuki, M., Marsh, H. W., & Lichtenfeld, S. (2016). Don't aim too high for your kids: Parental overaspiration undermines students' learning in mathematics. *Journal of Personality and Social Psychology*, *111*(5), 766–779. https://doi.org/10.1037/pspp0000079

Perszyk, D. R., & Waxman, S. R. (2018). Linking language and cognition in infancy. *Annual Review of Psychology*, *69*(1), 231–250. https://doi.org/10.1146/annurev-psych-122216-011701

Sun, R. C. F., & Hui, E. K. P. (2012). Cognitive competence as a positive youth development construct: A conceptual review. *The Scientific*

World Journal, *2012*, 1–7. https://doi.org/10.1100/2012/210953

The power of exploratory learning for young children. (2018, October 18). Galileo. https://galileo-camps.com/why-galileo/blog/the-power-of-exploratory-learning-for-young-children/

The Wright Flyer: From Invention to Icon. (n.d.). Smithsonian National Air and Space Museum. https://airandspace.si.edu/exhibitions/wright-brothers/online/icon/1903.cfm

What is a healthy level of expectation for your child? | st peter's prep. (2020, September 30). St Peter's Preparatory School. https://stpetersprep.co.uk/other-news/what-is-healthy-level-expectation-for-your-child/

Why exploration is essential for early education. (2019, April 24). Littleseedsofcarrollgardens.net. http://littleseedsofcarrollgardens.net/why-exploration-is-essential-for-early-education/

Wright, P. M., Hollenbeck, J. R., Wolf, S., & McMahan, G. C. (1995). The effects of varying goal difficulty operationalizations on goal setting outcomes and processes. *Organizational Behavior and Human Decision Processes*, *61*(1), 28–43. https://doi.org/10.1006/obhd.1995.1003

Zohar, A., & Tamir, P. (1993). Incorporating critical thinking into a regular high school biology curriculum. *School Science and Mathematics*, *93*(3), 136–140. https://doi.org/10.1111/j.1949-8594.1993.tb12211.x

www.ingramcontent.com/pod-product-compliance
Lightning Source LLC
LaVergne TN
LVHW051428080426
835508LV00022B/3291

9 7 8 1 9 5 6 0 1 8 2 2 6